WHAT WOULD JONATHAN WEAR?

The Snazzy Paper Doll Book

BY JONATHAN FONG

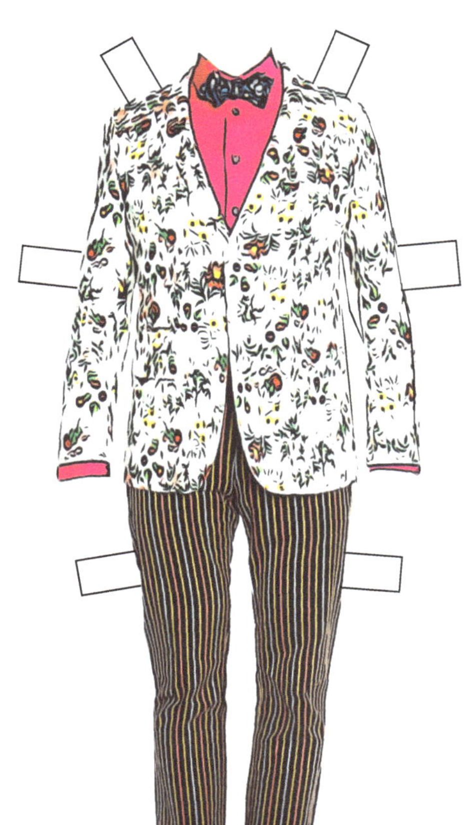

Printed in the United States of America

First Printing, 2019

ISBN 978-0-578-60566-1

Jonathan's figure illustration by mariadesigns & crotopus/fiverr
Gershwin and Fosse illustrations by mariadesigns/fiverr
Clothing illustrations and cover design by Jonathan Fong

www.jonathanfongstyle.com

INSTRUCTIONS

- Cut out the Jonathan figure on the inside front cover, being sure to include the stand.
- Don't bother cutting out the white gap under his arms or his legs. Just keep that portion solid.
- Fold the stand where the dotted lines are to help the figure stand up.
- To reinforce the stand, cut the easel out, folding along the dotted line, and attach it to the back of the figure with double-sided tape or a glue stick.
- Cut the clothes as you did the figure, keeping the white gaps between the arms and legs intact. Really, who has time for all that fussy cutting?

I'M REALLY A WALLFLOWER.
BUT I LIKE MY WALLS BRIGHT.

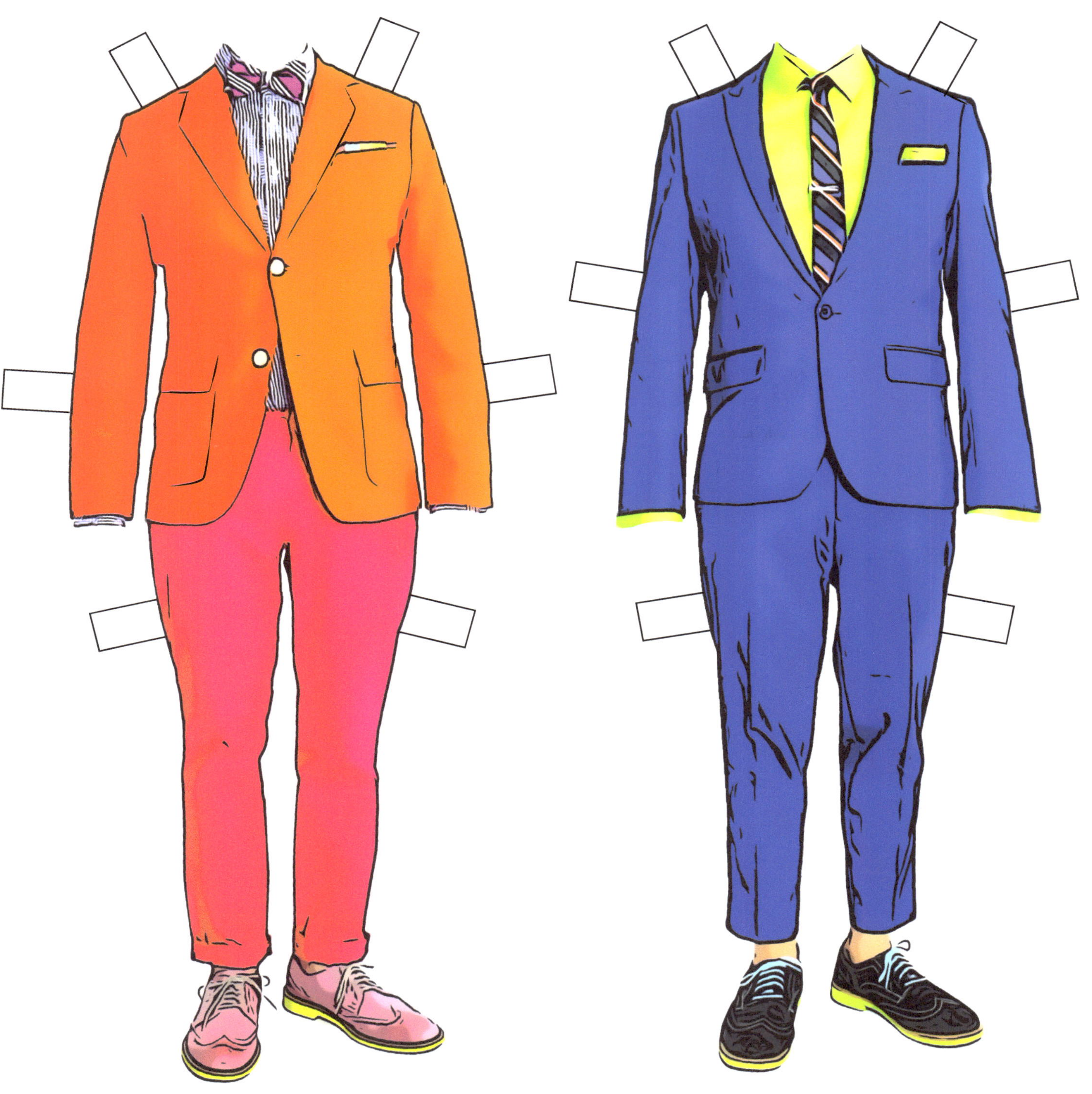

My favorite colors have changed through the years. Right now, they're pink and orange. And the two in combination make me very happy.

I love wearing suits. With a tie bar and a pocket square, I feel like I have superpowers.

LIFE'S YOUR STAGE.
ALWAYS BE IN COSTUME.

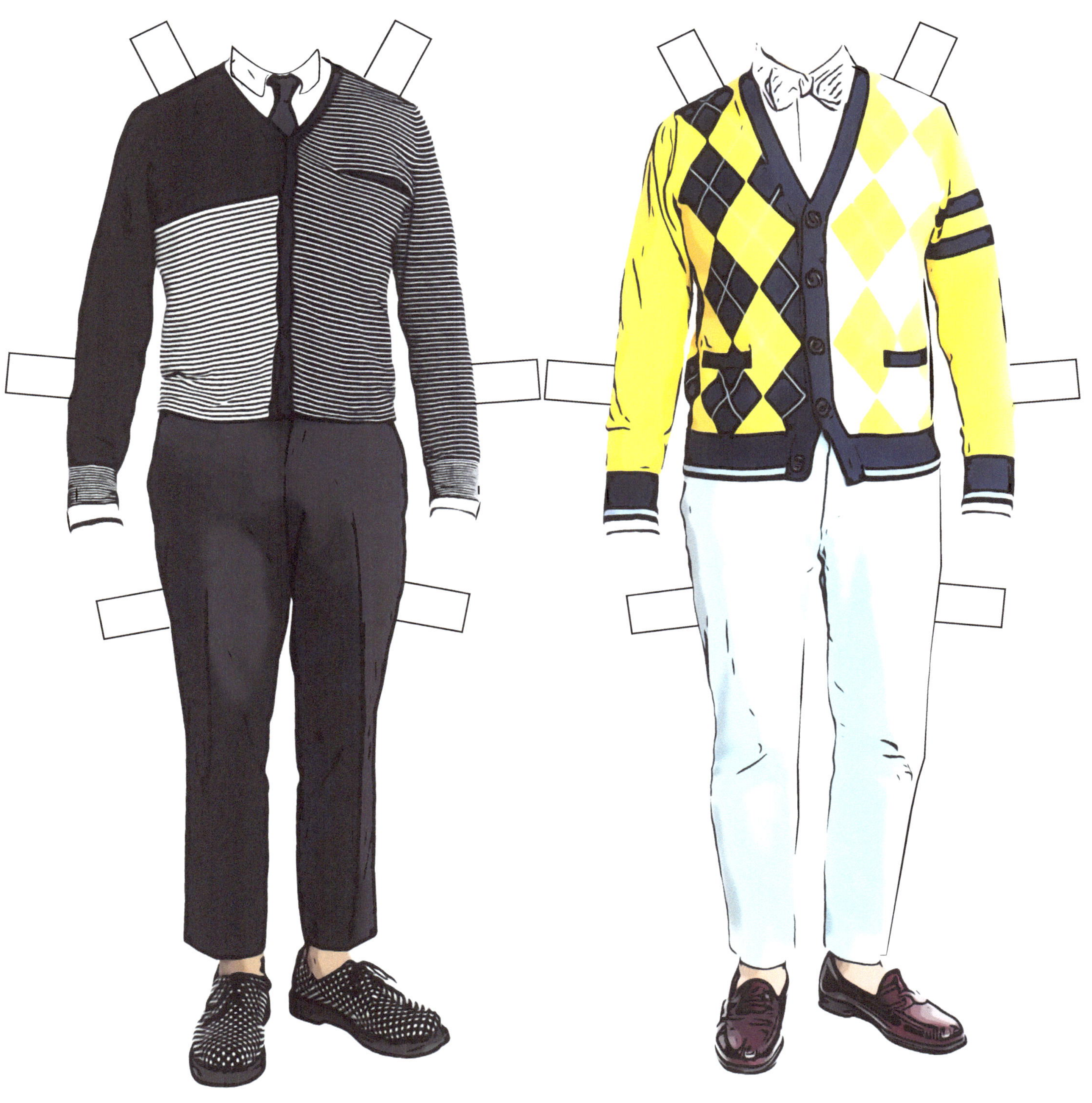

This cardigan used to be really long, so I hemmed it, even though my sewing skills are pretty basic. If you can see the imperfections, you're too close.

I always say yes to argyle.
Because diamonds are also a guy's best friend.

IT'S CALLED STYLE.
GOOGLE IT.

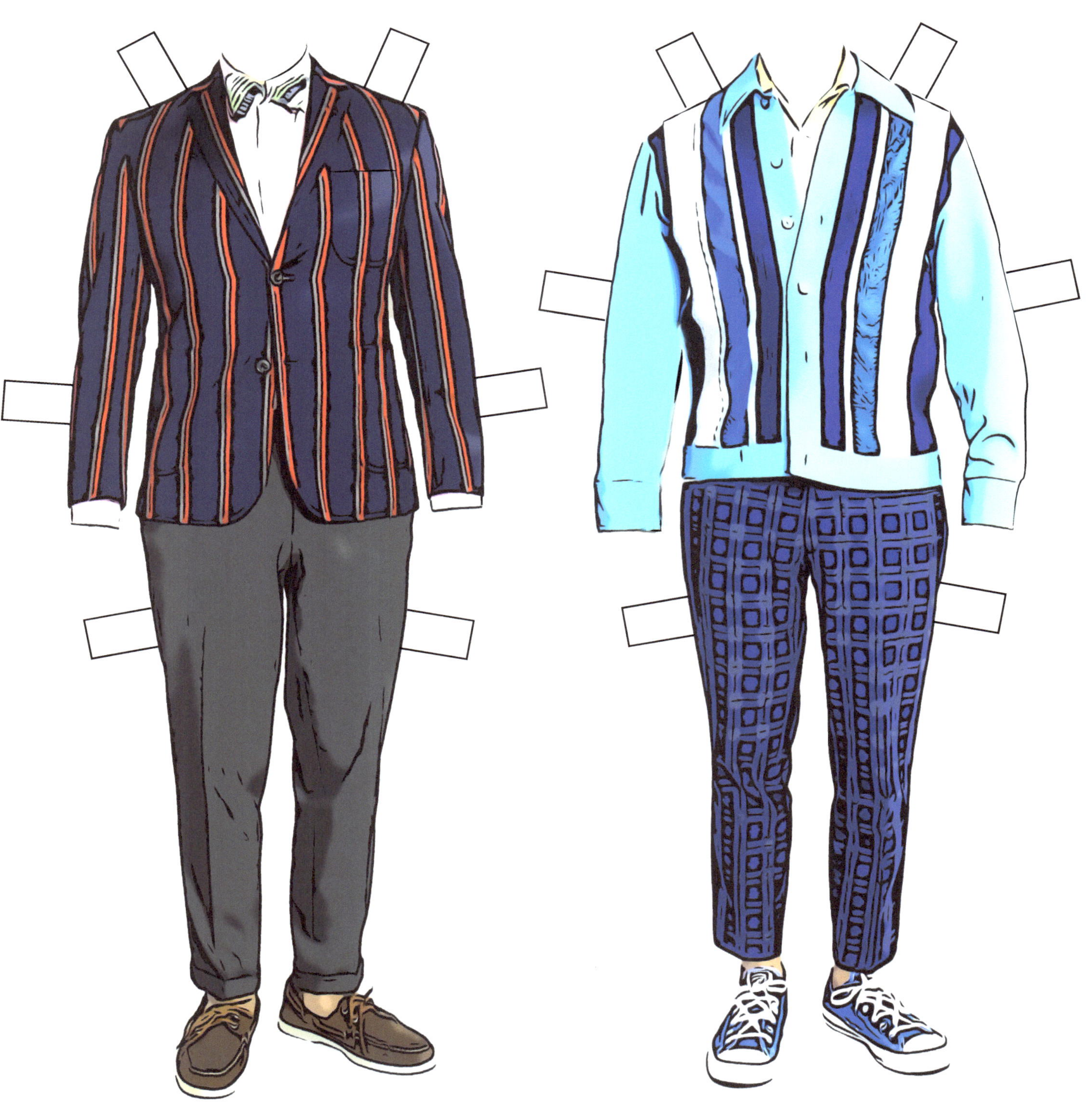

I learned how to tie a bow tie by watching a YouTube tutorial. For the first 20 times or so, I had to watch the video first. I think I finally have the hang of it.

I enjoy vintage clothes shopping because I love the idea of an article of clothing being passed on to another generation and another user. The story goes on.

ALWAYS DRESS AS IF
THE PAPARAZZI WERE HIDING
IN THE BUSHES.

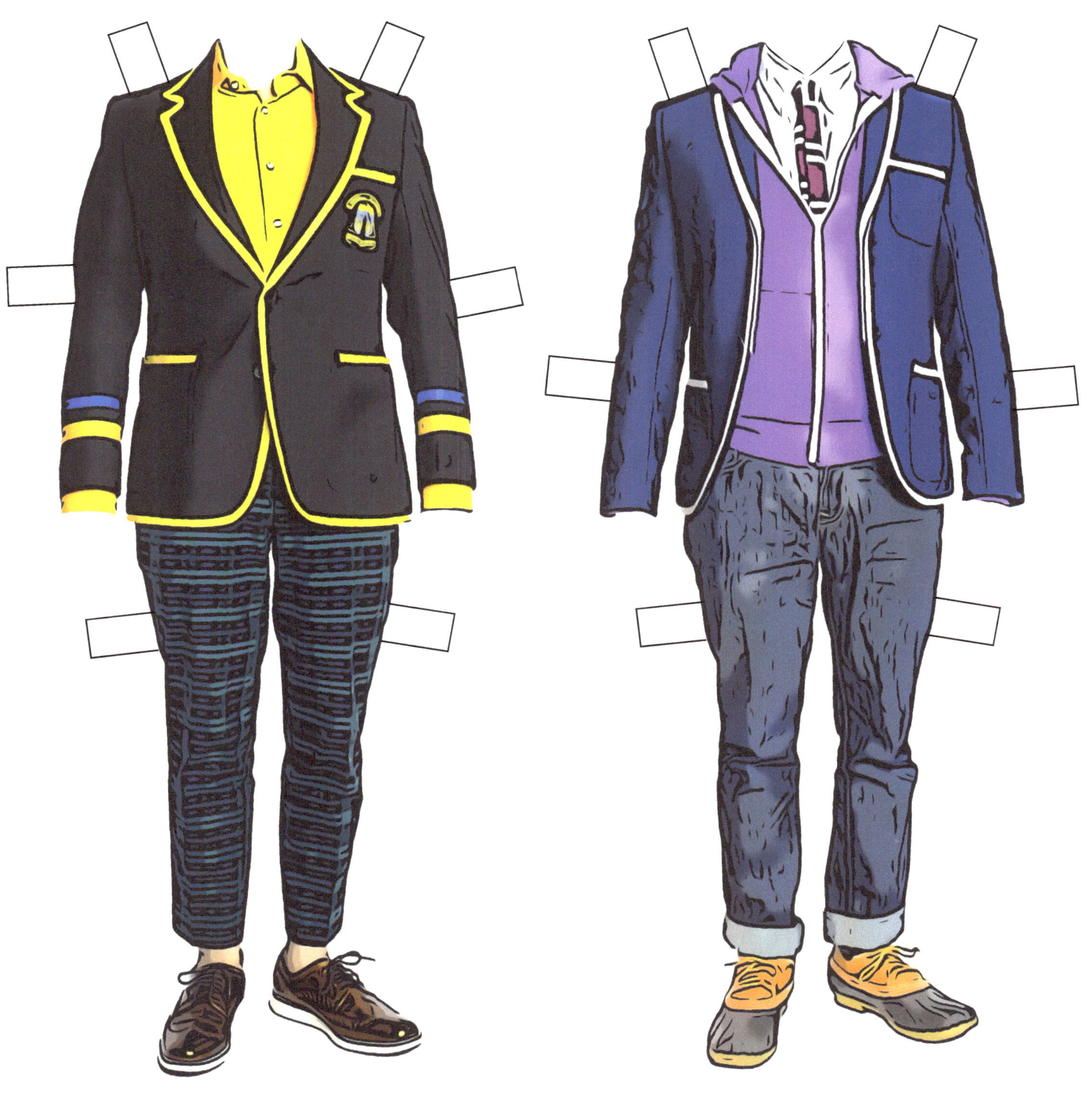

I have no problem buying clothes online.
This blazer is a vintage school uniform I found on eBay.

These duck boots from L.L. Bean are from my college days. I went to graduate school in Boston, so I had them in every height.

I'D RATHER BE UNDRESSED THAN UNDERDRESSED.

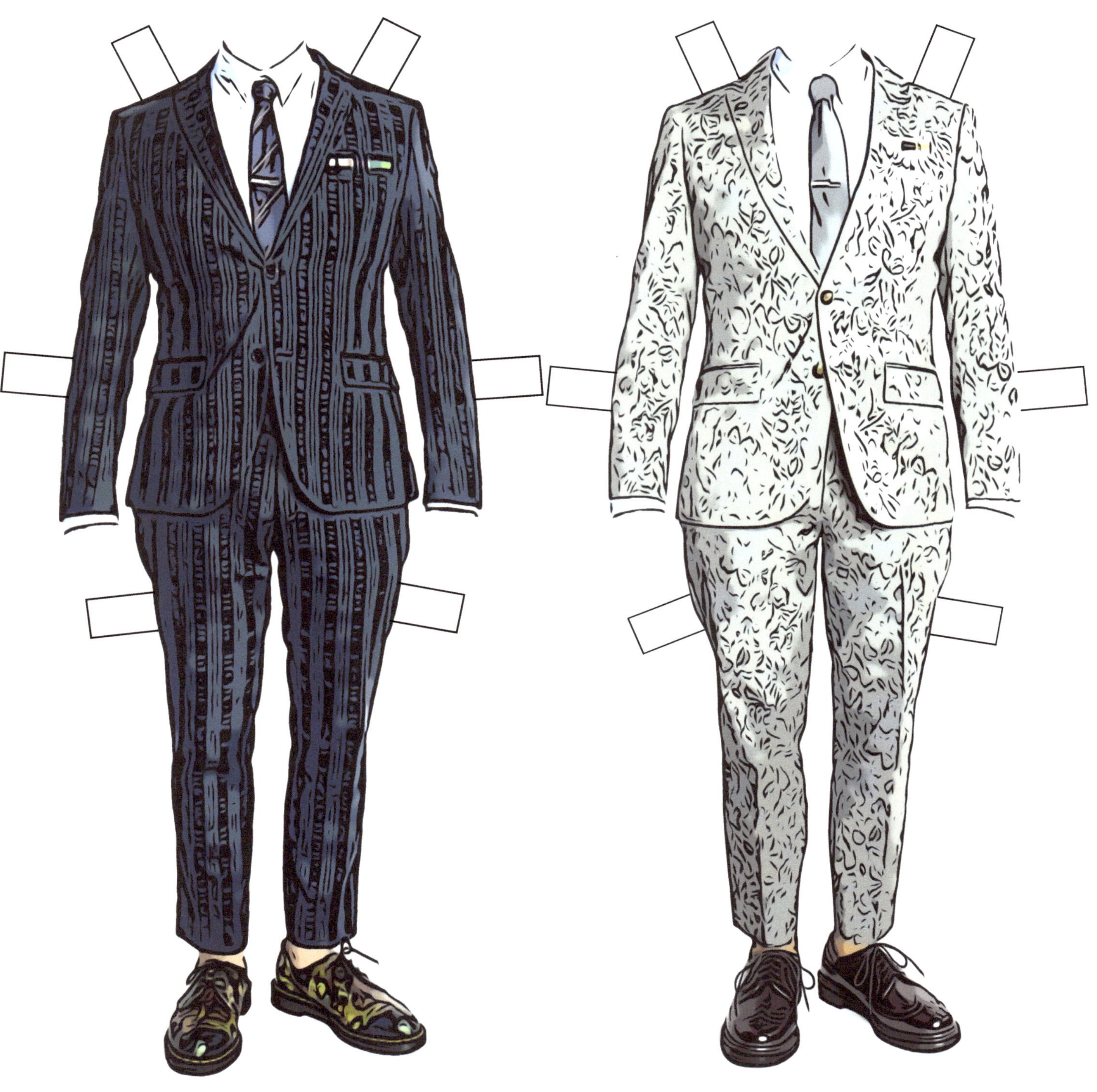

Suits don't fit me perfectly off the rack. The arms and the pants are usually too long, so I have them altered at my local tailor. Tailors make you look good.

I realize I wear my pants shorter than most people. I just find that when they're longer and break on my shoes, they look sloppy. And I like showing a little ankle.

IT DOESN'T MATTER WHO WEARS THE PANTS IN THE FAMILY AS LONG AS THEY'RE FABULOUS.

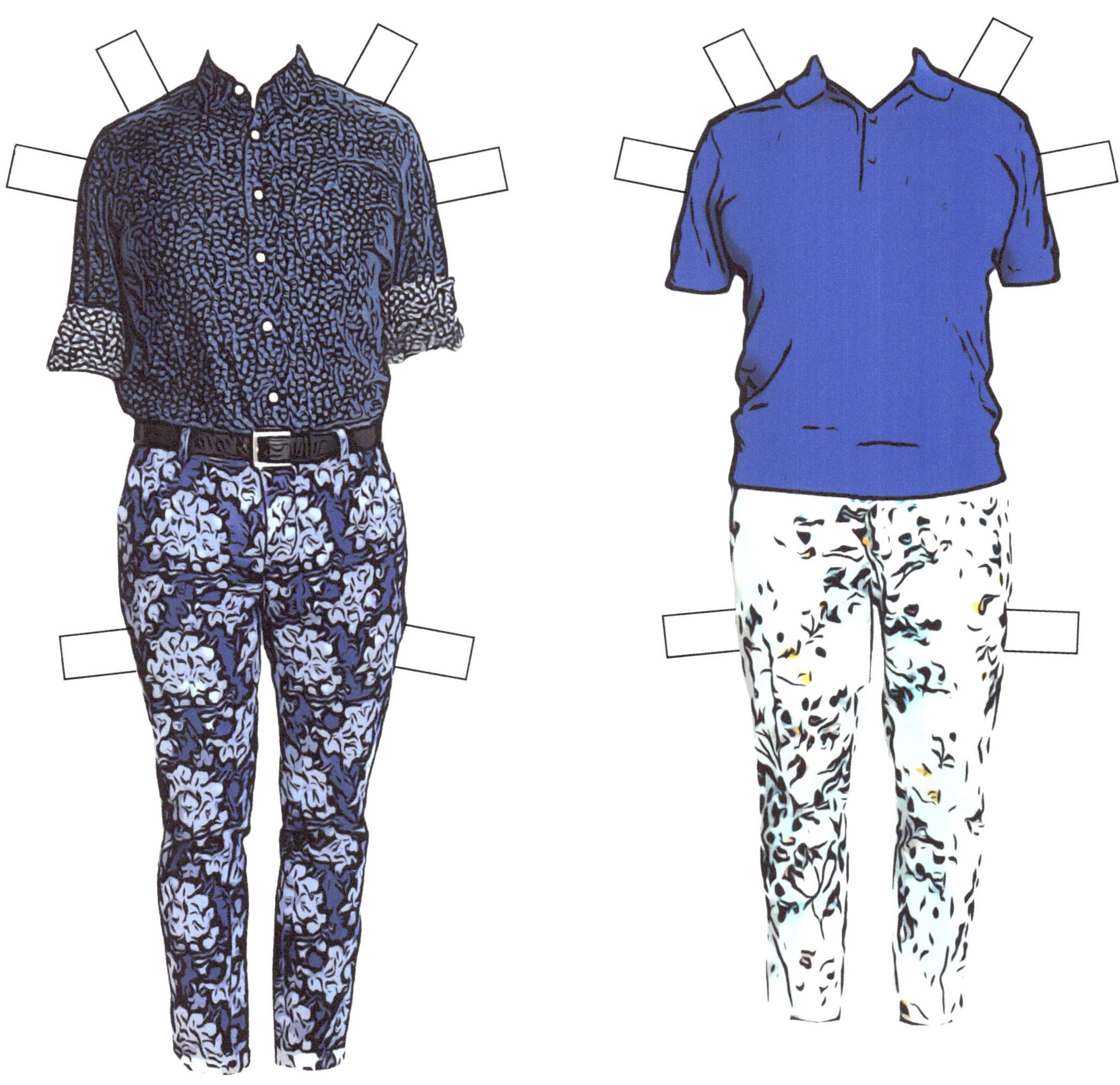

Floral pants are so much fun to wear.
If you're shy about wearing florals, go monochromatic with them like I did here.

I used to be very self-conscious about showing my scrawny arms in short sleeve shirts.
Now I embrace my ectomorph form.

I'VE NEVER MET A PLAID
I DIDN'T LIKE.

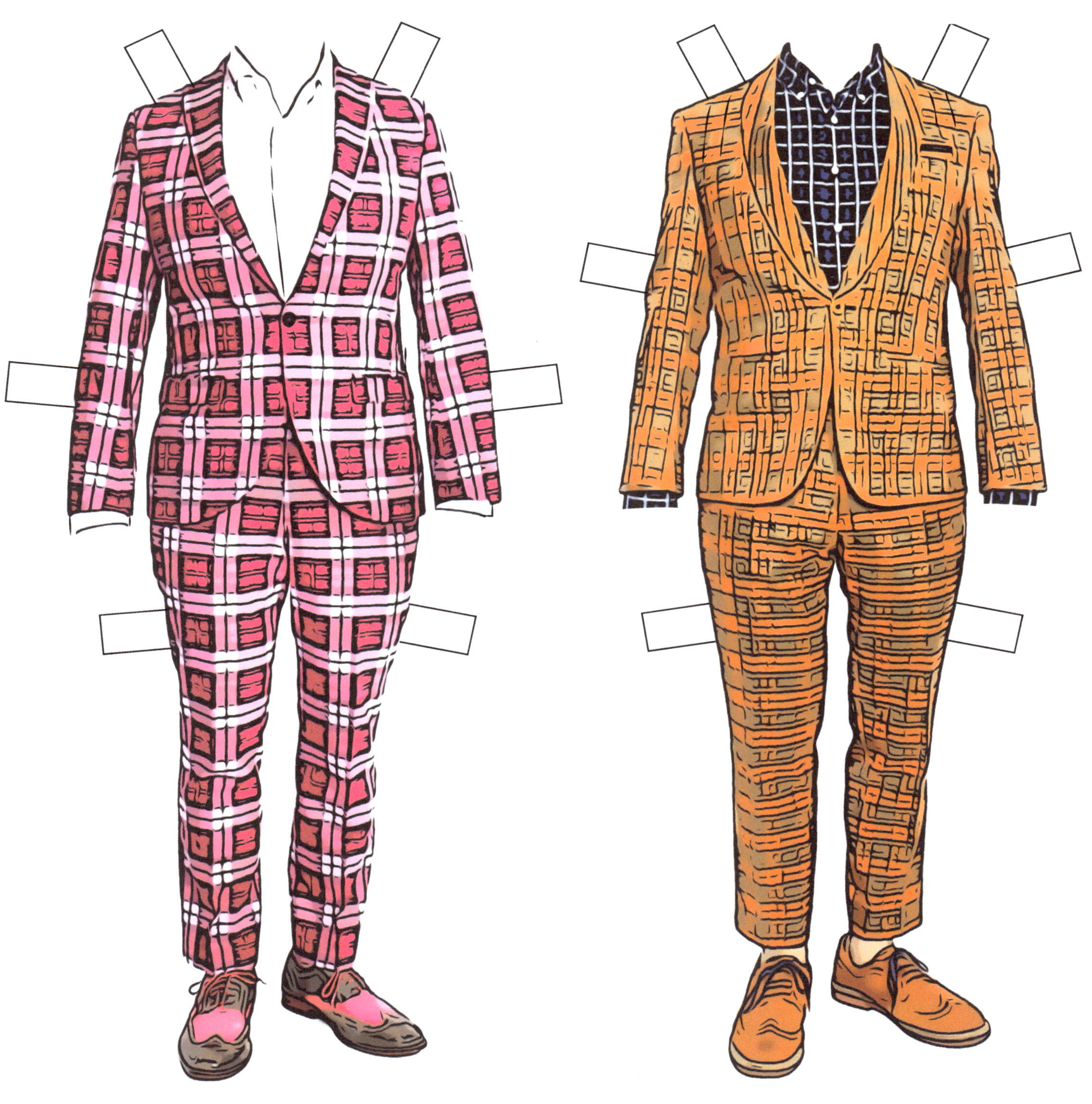

Plaid suits used to be associated with used car salesmen.
I don't think any car salesman had a pink one like this.

I'm not sure why I'm so mad for plaid.
Maybe I was Scottish in a former life.

DRESS UP JUST IN CASE
YOU RUN INTO YOUR EX.

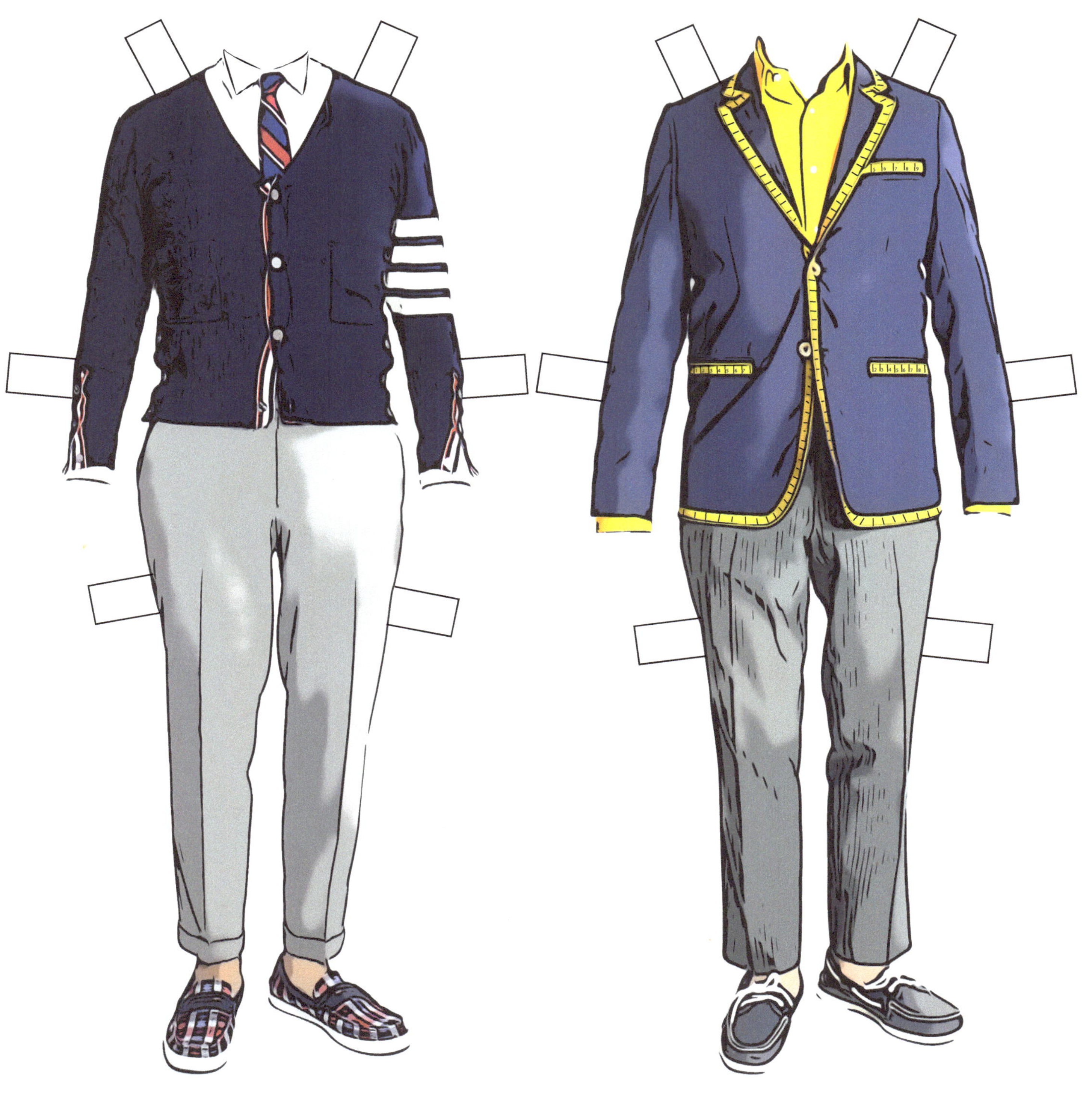

It's fun to wear a tie when you don't have to.

This was a blazer that I embellished with measuring tape trim. It's one of my favorite clothing makeovers.

IT'S BETTER TO BE STARED AT THAN IGNORED.

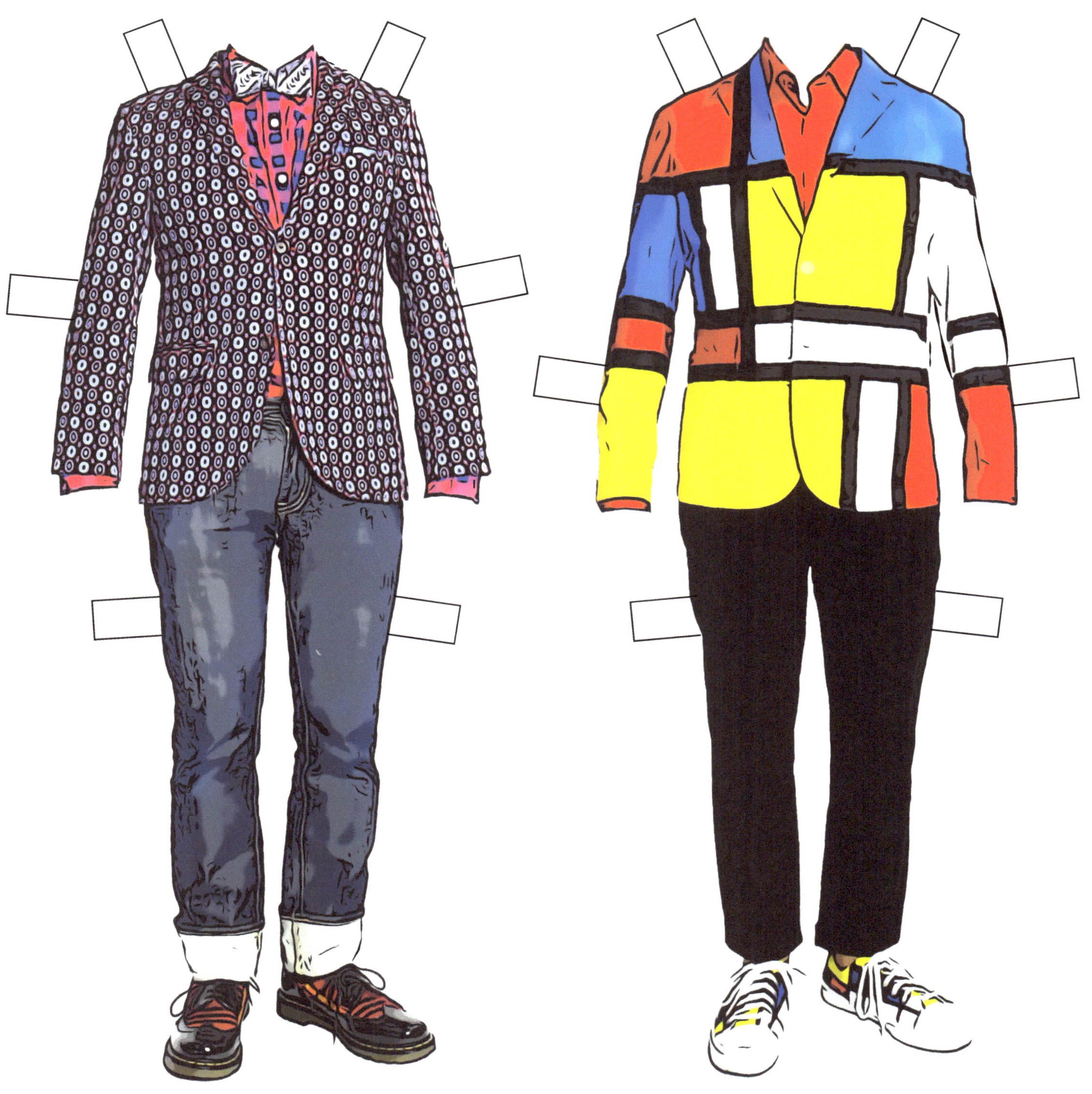

Mixing patterns is a lot of fun, and I don't care if they clash a little. For me, it's like mixing furniture styles — if you like the pieces, go for it.

Inspired by the iconic Yves Saint Laurent dress, I painted this Mondrian pattern on a plain white blazer, and I created the matching shoes.

I PINK, THEREFORE I AM.

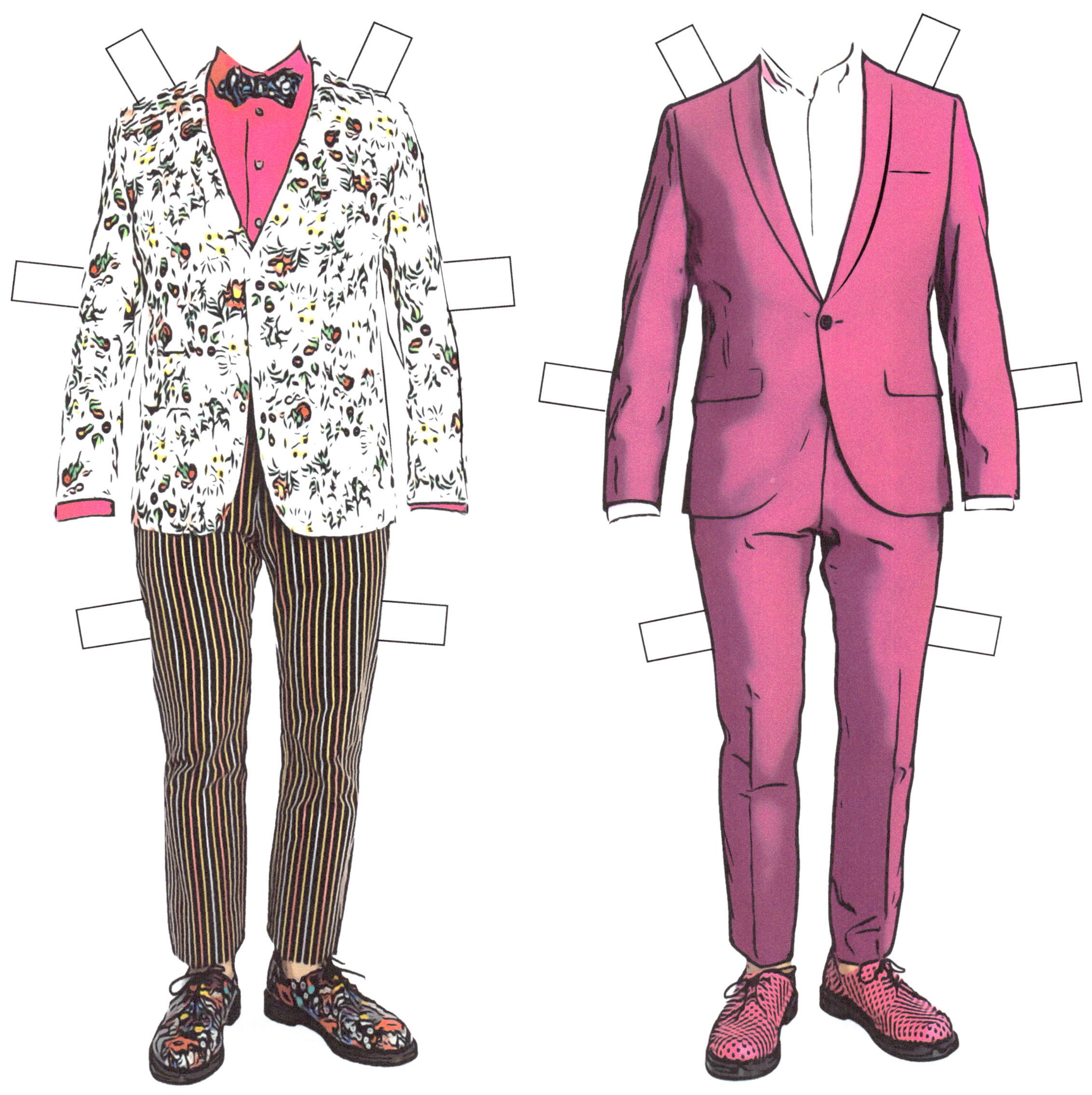

Some say you've got to be confident to wear a floral blazer. I say it gives me confidence.

Pink was originally a color associated with boys. It wasn't until the 1940s that manufacturers decided to market pink clothing to girls.

SOMETIMES LESS IS MORE.
BUT SOMETIMES MORE IS MORE.

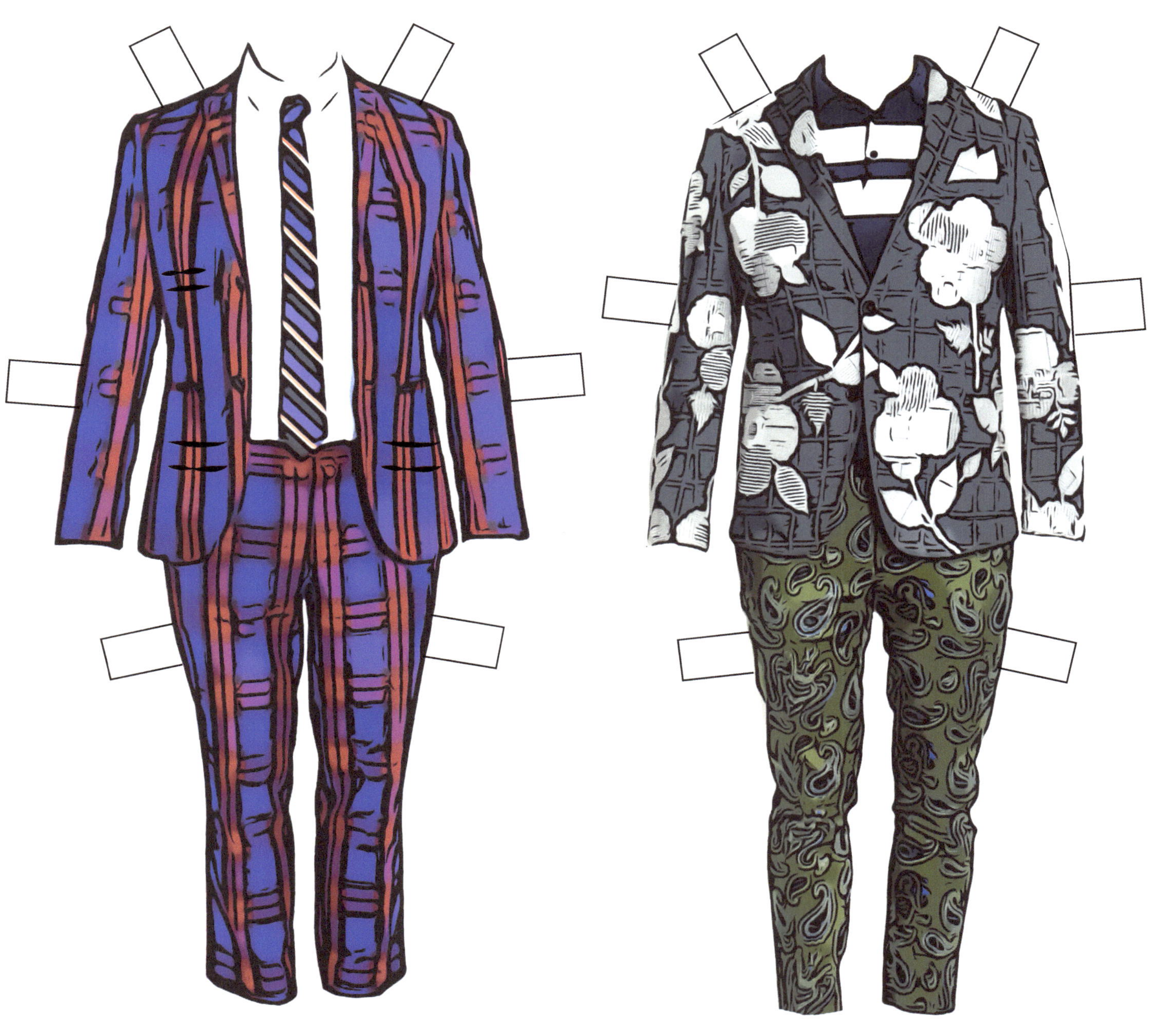

I rarely wear a belt with a suit. I feel like it breaks up the vertical line of the suit and chops my body in half.

Another DIY blazer makeover, I embellished this plain jacket with diecut iron-on patches I created with Sizzix floral dies by Eileen Hull.

BEING NORMAL
IS SO LAST SEASON.

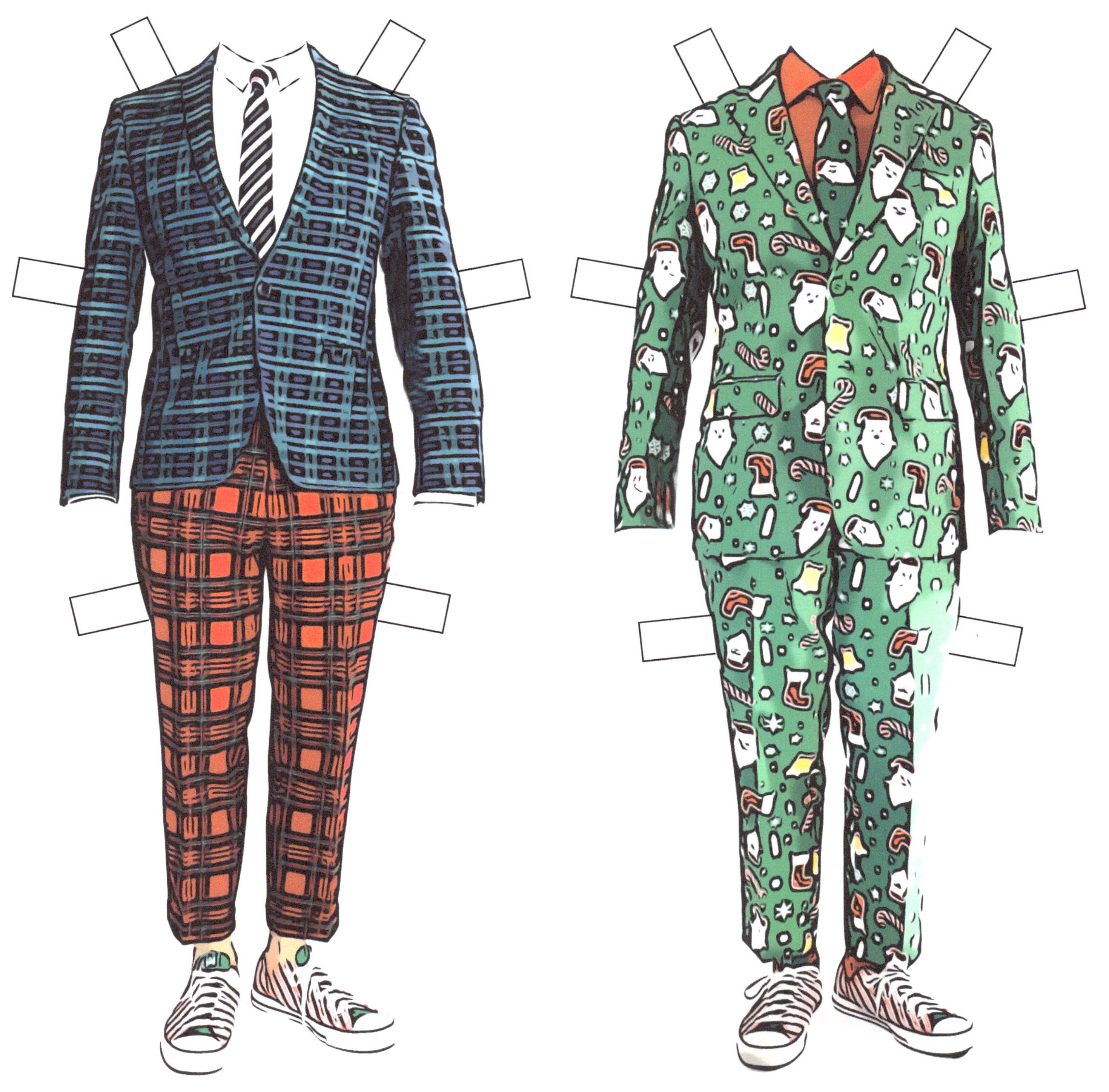

Salesperson: Would you like the green or red plaid?
Me: Yes, please.

I guess I do like to make an entrance at a holiday party.

www.ingramcontent.com/pod-product-compliance
Lightning Source LLC
Chambersburg PA
CBHW041115050726
47599CB00003BB/650

* 9 7 8 0 5 7 8 6 0 5 6 6 1 *